IDA B. WELLS

MARCHES FOR THE VOTE

IDA B. WELLS

MARCHES FOR THE VOTE

Written by

DINAH JOHNSON

Illustrated by

JERRY JORDAN

Christy Ottaviano Books

LITTLE, BROWN AND COMPANY
New York Boston

ABOUT THIS BOOK

The illustrations for this book were done in oil on canvas. This book was edited by Christy Ottaviano and designed by Patrick Collins and Véronique Lefèvre Sweet with art direction from Saho Fujii. The production was supervised by Kimberly Stella, and the production editors were Jen Graham and Annie McDonnell. The text was set in LTC Pabst Oldstyle, and the display type is Blackriver.

Text copyright © 2024 by Dinah Johnson • Illustrations copyright © 2024 by Jerry Jordan • Cover illustration © 2024 by Jerry Jordan • Cover design by Patrick Collins • Cover copyright © 2024 by Hachette Book Group, Inc. • Hachette Book Group supports the right to free expression and the value of copyright. The purpose of copyright is to encourage writers and artists to produce the creative works that enrich our culture. • The scanning, uploading, and distribution of this book without permission is a theft of the author's intellectual property. If you would like permission to use material from the book (other than for review purposes), please contact permissions@hbgusa.com. Thank you for your support of the author's rights. • Christy Ottaviano Books • Hachette Book Group • 1290 Avenue of the Americas, New York, NY 10104 • Visit us at LBYR.com • First Edition: January 2024 • Christy Ottaviano Books is an imprint of Little, Brown and Company. • The Christy Ottaviano Books name and logo are trademarks of Hachette Book Group, Inc. • The publisher is not responsible for websites (or their content) that are not owned by the publisher. • Photos courtesy of the Hanna Holborn Gray Special Collections Research Center, University of Chicago Library; stamp "Black Heritage: Ida B. Wells (1990) United States Postal Service®. All rights reserved. Used with permission." • Little, Brown and Company books may be purchased in bulk for business, educational, or promotional use. For information, please contact your local bookseller or the Hachette Book Group Special Markets Department at special.markets@hbgusa.com. • Library of Congress Cataloging-in-Publication Data • Names: Johnson, Dinah, author. | Jordan, Jerry, illustrator. • Title: Marching for the vote : Ida B. Wells and the Women's March of 1913 / by Dinah Johnson ; illustrated by Jerry Jordan. • Other titles: Ida B. Wells and the Women's March of 1913 • Description: First edition. | New York : Little, Brown and Company, 2023. | Includes bibliographical references. | Audience: Ages 5–9 | Summary: "A picture book biography about Ida B. Wells and her life as a suffragist, with a focus on the Women's March of 1913." —Provided by publisher. • Identifiers: LCCN 2022017892 | ISBN 9780316322478 (hardcover) • Subjects: LCSH: Wells-Barnett, Ida B., 1862–1931—Juvenile literature. | African American women civil rights workers—Biography—Juvenile literature. | Women—Suffrage—Washington (D.C.)—History—20th century—Juvenile literature. | Women—Suffrage—United States—History—Juvenile literature. | Suffragists—United States—Juvenile literature. | Civil rights workers—United States—Biography—Juvenile literature. | United States—Race relations—Juvenile literature. | African Americans—Civil rights—History—Juvenile literature. | African American women journalists—Biography—Juvenile literature. | African Americans—Social conditions—To 1964—Juvenile literature. • Classification: LCC E185.97. W55 J64 2023 | DDC 323.092 • [B]—dc23/eng/20220527 • LC record available at https://lccn.loc.gov/2022017892 • ISBN 978-0-316-32247-8 • PRINTED IN CHINA • APS • 10 9 8 7 6 5 4 3 2 1

For my great-aunt Pauline Young and for my aunts Quinnie Lee Gilliard,
Beatrice Townsend Johnson, Mildred Samuel, and Rosemary Wiggs

For my othermothers, Mary Thomas, Mary Justice,
Verdell Roberts, and Joan Warshauer Fox

For scholars Joyce Hansen, Shirley Geiger, Tera Hunter, and Wanda Hendricks,
who shared her expertise and encouragement as I marched into this project

For the inspiring women of Delta Sigma Theta Sorority, Inc.
and for my Delta friends, too numerous to name

For a few special Deltas—
my sisterfriends Laquita Blockson and Angela Kiper Poe,
my sister, Debora Johnson-Ross, and my sister-in-law, Sonia Gass

And most of all
for my beloved mother and father—
Beatrice Taylor Johnson and Douglas L. Johnson Sr.,
dedicated sister of Delta Sigma Theta Sorority, Inc.,
dedicated brother of Omega Psi Phi Fraternity, Inc.—
in celebration of lives well lived, in service, in beauty, in love
—DJ

To my family for their love and support and believing in me.
Especially my wife, Nyra
—JJ

Ida B. Wells was born on July 16, 1862, in the Southern state of Mississippi. Just months later, on January 1, 1863, the Emancipation Proclamation freed enslaved people in the South. Ida's parents must have been overjoyed that they would raise their young family in freedom.

But it was not a perfect freedom. Black people, whose ancestors were from the continent of Africa, still did not have the right to vote, though they were Americans too.

When the Fifteenth Amendment was ratified in 1870 and Black men could vote, Ida's father marched, with his head held high, to cast his ballot. His boss was so angry that he fired Ida's father.

Mr. Wells knew what he had to do. He opened a carpentry shop and worked for himself.

Ida was a little girl when that happened. As she grew older, she saw her parents always stand up for what was right. So it is not surprising that Ida always tried to do the right thing too, fighting for her family and for her community to be treated with dignity.

Sadly, she was just a teenager when her mother, father, and baby brother died from a disease called yellow fever.

Ida and her brothers and sisters were thankful they could stay in the home their parents worked so hard to build for them.

Her brothers and sisters were growing up quickly.

Because they needed food and clothes and maybe a little treat once in a while, Ida had to grow up even more quickly to provide for them.

Ida loved words and books and learning, and she had
always excelled at her schoolwork. Ida was prepared to
do the right thing.

Though she was still a teenager, Ida began teaching students of her own. That way, she could earn money to take care of her family while also helping others learn to read and write.

The years went by, and soon Ida was an adult. She kept on doing the right thing, even if that thing was scary or hard to do. There was the time when she was riding on a train, minding her own business. Because of the color of her skin, the conductor forced her to give up the first-class seat she had bought.

Ida fought back in the courtroom, standing tall and telling her story to a judge. What a brave thing to do.

When Black people were being lynched—killed by gangs of white people angry that slavery was abolished—Ida B. Wells began writing articles in her very own newspaper. Her words were so powerful that people all over the country listened and trusted her opinion.

She wrote feverishly and published her editorials anywhere
possible because she wanted everyone to know what was happening.
That was the truthful thing to do.

Ida even traveled all the way to England to give speeches so that people around the world would learn about some of the frightening things happening in the United States of America. That was a bold thing to do.

As difficult as life was sometimes, Ida worked tirelessly because she believed that change was possible.

CHICAGO

By now she lived in Chicago. Her husband, Ferdinand Barnett, was a lawyer who believed, just as much as Ida did, that life would get better. They both worked hard to encourage people to treat everyone as they themselves would like to be treated. Most importantly, Ida and Ferdinand worked to change laws that were unjust.

They wanted their children to live in an America that was fair to everybody, an America where not just white people, and not just men, had the right to vote. Ida and Ferdinand had hopes that their daughters and sons would live in an America where women could vote in every city and in every state.

Ida knew that hopes and dreams were important. She also knew that hope was not enough all by itself. People had to take action. So she organized the Alpha Suffrage Club.

The women of the Alpha Suffrage Club had a goal for Black women to be able to vote, to choose the people who would speak for their community when big decisions were being made.

They believed deeply that there would be a time when all women could vote in every election, not only in Chicago but across the United States.

Perhaps one day, Ida's youngest daughter, Alfreda, would march with the grown-up women, even if she had to take big steps to keep up with her mother.

Ida B. Wells must have been thinking about Alfreda when she went to Washington, DC—the National American Woman Suffrage Association, which allowed only white women to be members, had organized a parade to be held there. Women came from all over the country to lift their voices as one.

There were over five thousand marchers in the nation's capital on March 3, 1913. Some of them would walk with friends who had traveled from the same cities and states they represented. Others would march alongside women who did similar kinds of work. There were nurses and teachers, librarians and homemakers, lawyers and artists, and more.

Lined up at the head of the parade was a suffragette riding a stately horse. Behind her was the first of many floats. On it was a banner that read: *We demand an amendment to the Constitution of the United States enfranchising the women of this country.*

For the women holding the banner, those words meant that they
wanted the vote only for white women, those whose ancestors came from
Europe. They did not care about African American, Asian American, or
Mexican American women. They were not concerned about Indigenous
women, whose ancestors were the first to live on this land.

Alice Paul, one of the white women who had planned the
march, believed that people should only be with those who
looked like them. She had made the despicable statement
"We must have a white procession, or a Negro procession,
or no procession at all."

Yet a small number of Black women from all over the country did the bold thing. They got in line to march with the white women of their states.

Marching with dignity at the back of the parade was the famous, fearless Black suffragette Mary Church Terrell. She was with the courageous young women of Delta Sigma Theta Sorority of Howard University. This was the first public activity they participated in as a group. They knew they had to march for the vote if Black people in America, both men and women, were to have a future bright with promise.

Ida B. Wells was a proud Delta too. The women of Delta Sigma Theta, along with some of the members of the Alpha Suffrage Club, did not let Alice Paul's racism change their minds. All of them were determined to march that day with their heads held high.

Some of the women of the national organizing committee for the march, and even some of the Illinois delegation, thought that Ida B. Wells should march at the back of the parade alongside her sorority sisters.

Ida admired her sisters, but she had other ideas.

She paid no attention to the white women who argued and argued. When they finally stopped talking—it was time to get in their own places and start the parade—these quarreling white women had a big surprise.

Ida B. Wells was nowhere in sight.

Ever since she was a young woman, Ida had always done the right thing. The right thing now was *not* to follow the wishes of these white women who didn't care if she and other Black women got the vote.

The right thing now was for Ida to follow her heart and mind. She worked her way through the crowds of people along the path of the parade.

It might have been frightening to pass by men shouting and throwing things at the women marchers. Perhaps Ida stayed calm by thinking about her father, marching up to the ballot box so many years before.

Perhaps she looked at the grand buildings of Washington, DC, and thought about Woodrow Wilson's inauguration as president taking place the next day, and about what it meant to be an American.

Maybe she was thinking about Alfreda, and her entire family, who would want to hear all about the nation's capital and the big parade.

Step after step, maybe she thought about the children who would be born in twenty, fifty, one hundred years.

And then . . .

. . . with a suffragette friend on each side of her, Ida B. Wells followed her heart and mind as she stepped into the parade, joining the white women of the Illinois delegation.

One or two of them may have smiled. But those who had argued so loudly that she should stay at the back of the parade now said nothing at all.

And because Ida B. Wells always did the right thing, the brave and bold and truthful thing, she kept right on
            marching,
                  marching,
                        marching for the vote.

Ida B. Wells-Barnett
with her children, 1909

A Note from the Author

Ida B. Wells-Barnett never stopped fighting for people to be able to live their lives with basic human dignity.

Many Americans celebrated 2020 as the hundredth anniversary of the Nineteenth Amendment to the United States Constitution, which gave women the right to vote. But in actuality, Black Americans, both women and men, could not freely exercise this birthright until the passage of the Voting Rights Act of 1965. Unfortunately, Ida B. Wells-Barnett did not live to see that day. But throughout her life, she believed that day would come.

Both the civil rights movement and the women's rights movement in America are indebted to Ida B. Wells-Barnett and her tireless march for the vote and for equality. She was an important activist in the anti-lynching campaigns throughout the country as well. Her many invaluable contributions to society were celebrated in 1990 when the US Postal Service issued the Ida B. Wells commemorative stamp. More than a century after the Women's March of 1913, her story is as important and inspiring as ever.

Ida B. Wells-Barnett with
her daughters, Ida, thirteen,
and Alfreda, ten,
September 1914

Alfreda Barnett, Ida's
daughter, age sixteen

Ida B. Wells

25

Black Heritage USA

Timeline of the Life of Ida B. Wells-Barnett

1862   Ida B. Wells is born in Holly Springs, Mississippi, on July 16.

1877   Attends Shaw University (later renamed Rust College) in Holly Springs.

1878   Parents and baby brother die in a yellow fever epidemic.

Begins working as a teacher at age sixteen to support her family. Attends college between school terms.

1881   Moves to Memphis, Tennessee, and commutes by train to teach.

1883   Sues the Chesapeake, Ohio and Southwestern Railroad Company after being forcibly removed from the first-class ladies' car. She's awarded $500 in damages in 1884. The Tennessee Supreme Court will overturn the decision in 1887.

1885–1891   Writes for Black newspapers while teaching in Memphis schools.

1889   Becomes editor-in-chief and part owner of the Memphis weekly *Free Speech and Headlight* (also referred to as *The Memphis Free Press* and the *Memphis Free Press and Headlight*).

1892   Becomes active in the anti-lynching movement after a friend and two other men are lynched in Memphis. The offices of the *Free Speech and Headlight* are destroyed after Ida's anti-lynching editorials are published.

Gives lectures in New York, Boston, Philadelphia, and Washington, DC, on the truth about lynching.

1893 Travels to Britain and gives anti-lynching lectures in England and Scotland.

Publishes, with Frederick Douglass, the ninety-six-page pamphlet *The Reason Why the Colored American Is Not in the World's Columbian Exposition*, which is distributed at the World's Fair in Chicago.

1895 Publishes *A Red Record: Tabulated Statistics and Alleged Causes of Lynchings in the United States, 1892, 1893, 1894*.

Marries Ferdinand Barnett in Chicago. The wedding is announced in the *New York Times*, quite uncommon for Black Americans. Also uncommon at the time, she hyphenates her last name, Wells-Barnett. The couple goes on to have four children.

1896 Helps establish the National Association of Colored Women.

1898 Goes to the White House to demand that President William McKinley introduce anti-lynching reforms.

1898–1902 Serves as secretary of the National Afro-American Council.

1909 Participates in the conference that results in the creation of the NAACP, the National Association for the Advancement of Colored People.

1913 Founds Chicago's Alpha Suffrage Club, believed to be the first suffrage group for Black women.

Marches for the vote, both in Chicago and in Washington, DC.

1931 Dies of kidney disease at age sixty-eight on March 25 in Chicago. She was politically active all her life.

1970 *Crusade for Justice*, her life story in her own words, is published.

This timeline represents only a small amount of information about the activities of Ida B. Wells-Barnett, endless fighter for human rights. The sources listed in the bibliography offer greater insights and cite additional sources.

Sources

The story highlighted in this book during the Women's March of 1913 is an abridged peek into one incident in the amazing life of Ida B. Wells-Barnett. Two white suffragettes, Belle Squire and Virginia Brooks, did, in fact, march by her side in the national parade. The sources listed below will be informative and useful as you explore this incident, her career, and her life in a fuller, more contextualized way.

For Young Readers:

Dray, Philip. Illus. by Stephen Alcorn. *Yours for Justice, Ida B. Wells: The Daring Life of a Crusading Journalist.* Atlanta: Peachtree, 2008.

Fradin, Dennis Brindell, and Judith Bloom Fradin. *Ida B. Wells: Mother of the Civil Rights Movement.* New York: Clarion Books, 2000.

Myers, Walter Dean. *Ida B. Wells: Let the Truth Be Told.* New York: Amistad Press/HarperCollins, 2008.

For Adult Readers:

Ansah, Ama. "Votes for Women Means Votes for Black Women." National Women's History Museum. August 16, 2018. www.womenshistory.org/articles/votes-women-means-votes -black-women.

Giddings, Paula J. *Ida: A Sword Among Lions; Ida B. Wells and the Campaign Against Lynching.* New York: Amistad/HarperCollins, 2008.

Hendricks, Wanda A. *Gender, Race, and Politics in the Midwest: Black Club Women in Illinois.* Bloomington: Indiana University Press, 1998.